Sadhu Sundar Singh

He walked with God

Incorporating material first dictated by late Mr. N. Daniel
who personally knew Sundar Singh

Joshua Daniel

Laymen's Evangelical Fellowship International
London South Bend Detroit Chennai Bombay
Heidelberg Toronto Perth Georgetown

First Edition May 1988 (2,000 copies)
Second Edition (Revised) May 1990 (5,000 copies)
Third Edition (Improved and Enlarged)
   Copyright © 1996 Joshua Daniel
Reprinted May 1999 (4,000 copies)

ISBN 1-873523-16-5

For orders and other inquires, contact any of the addresses below:

Laymen's Evangelical Fellowship International
-P.O. Box 737, London SW2 4XT, U.K.
-P.O. Box 2884, South Bend, IN, 46624, USA
-9B Nungambakkam High Rd, Chennai 600034, INDIA
-P.O. Box 701 Station A, Toronto, Ont. M5W1G2, CAN
-Am Aukopf 4, 69118 Heidelberg, GERMANY
-30 Rue Nationale, 75013 Paris, FRANCE
-Glasürweg 7, 9475 Sevelen, SWITZERLAND
-P.O. Box 24, Tuart Hill, Perth 6939, W.AUSTRALIA
-P.O. Box 12185, Georgetown, GUYANA, S.AMERICA
-Bedok Central, P.O. Box 0453, Singapore 914602
-37 Persiaran Shahbandar, Taman Tambahan Krian VI, 34200 Parit Buntar, Perak, MALAYSIA
-P.O. Box 15002, New Road P.O., Sabon Gari, Kano, NIGERIA
-11-B Temple Tower, P-17A Ashutosh Chowdhury Avenue, Ballygunge Phari, Calcutta 700019, INDIA

Printed and Bound in Great Britain by
Cox & Wyman Ltd, Reading, Berkshire

Contents

Introduction

There are many in our world today who are genuinely puzzled by such phrases as, "the Lord spoke to me" or "the Lord visited me" or "the Lord asked me to do this or that." No apology at all is owing to any man for the use of these phrases, provided the user has had a real and clear-cut experience of God, which evidences itself through the transparency, beauty and joy which he manifests in his everyday life. Moreover, "the Lord said," "the Lord spoke to me saying," "thus saith the Lord" are key phrases of the Bible, which are meant to be our experience too, today.

Here, in this book, we give the reader one of the most compelling lives of the twentieth century. Sundar Singh made no pretence to scholarship and high learning. Earlier on in the 20th century, when vicious attacks on the authenticity and authority of the Bible and its relevance to the present day and time were being freely made everywhere, God raised this young man, who at the outset was virulent in his opposition to Christianity, yet who, on meeting Christ, became so like Him.

Wherever he went, garbed in his simple saffron attire, and expressing himself in terms and phrases which a child could understand, Sundar Singh threw men into inexpressible wonder that he so closely resembled Jesus Christ in his life and walk. The manner in which the Lord Jesus revealed Himself to this young man who bitterly hated Him and the startling results which followed, shook even rabid sceptics and those who in the name of modern science and scholarship deride the supernatural.

It has been readily acknowledged by those who have ventured to write the life of Sundar Singh in the last two decades, that they had little access to any original matter. Some of them however did a tremendous job in trying to interpret this great man of God to a present-day generation, which scarcely understands the ABCs of spiritual life. Nearly all of these good and godly authors laboured under the decided disadvantage of not being able to converse with someone who knew Sundar Singh firsthand. While this book makes no claims to scholarship, it fills that gap, revealing Sundar Singh as a very human personality and as a young man saw him. That young man was my dad, who bore indelibly in his life, many marks of those precious lessons in Christlikeness, which he learned from Sadhu Sundar Singh.

Some of those golden threads of communion with God, holiness unto the Lord and complete obedience to His Word, which were richly woven into the texture of Sundar Singh's life, became a continuous weave in the life of my father also. But that is another story.*

Soon after my father's own conversion as a boy of sixteen, Sundar Singh's emergence and news of his love and exploits for Christ, came as balm to his soul and he longed to see him. This desire God gave him and more. Dad accompanied him and lived with him for some days.

Late in my dad's life he commenced dictating an account of Sundar Singh's life. He did not, however, manage to complete it, partly due to the lack of someone who could take down his dictation, amidst his heavy schedule. The

*That story can be read in the book "Another Daniel" by the same author.

incomplete narrative which he left behind, I have sought to complete.

It is amazing how Sundar Singh's life has captured the imagination and stirred a spirit of inquiry in millions of people. It is all the more remarkable that this sustained interest in his life and the lessons of his life have so persisted in all the continents, in spite of the paucity of the books written about him and their limited availability. It appears all the more incredible that this interest in Sundar Singh persists even today, after the passage of over sixty years since he was last heard of, before disappearing in the snows of the Himalayas, on what proved to be the last of his nearly twenty missionary journeys to Tibet. Thus many earnest and interested people will welcome the fresh light and the new intimate and authentic incidents from his life, which this book provides.

Our prayer is that God will speak to you through this short account of Sundar Singh's vibrant and Christlike life and cause you, like him, to seek the unsearchable riches which are in the Lord Jesus.

– Joshua Daniel

1

"Why Doesn't the Living God Work amongst Us Today?"

Now this was the question which haunted my dad in his early teen-age years. In Sundar Singh God provided a meaningful answer.

My late father, in his agonized quest to find reality, power and relevance in today's Christianity, was hardly given any convincing answers by the religious leaders around him. They failed to show him a faith which really produced answers. At this rather critical juncture in his youth, news reached him of one named Sundar Singh, who closely resembled Christ in His walk and life. He was thrilled to hear of his amazing conversion and of the mighty works God was doing in Sundar Singh's life. Sensing that here was one who really walked with God, he was greatly stirred.

Next he longed to meet Sundar Singh in person. At that time, my dad who was about seventeen years old, had himself been converted a little earlier. He had neither the finance nor the possibility of undertaking a long journey, from the Southern town of Kakinada where he was a student, to the Punjab in the North of India, to meet this wonderful and eclectic person. Thus my dad prayed, "Lord, bring this servant of Yours to my place." The Lord brought Sundar Singh to Kakinada within six months. My dad was even then learning a life of prayer, with single-mindedness in this quiet rural town.

It happened this way. One day he heard that Sundar Singh was going to visit his place. His excitement and joy at the prospect of meeting this great man of God was unbounded. Such was his earnestness, zeal and practical turn of mind that he wanted all of his friends and class-mates to hear Sundar Singh. Some of them were proud and indifferent, and despised anything that had to do with the 'Christian' religion, such as the sort which they saw around them. He even besought some of them upon his knees, to go and hear Sundar Singh. Many of them did.

Sundar Singh's words made a profound impression upon them all. One of them said to my dad, soon after having a meeting with Sundar Singh "Daniel, I can never be the same again: I am a Christian from this day." He turned to Christ from Hinduism and during his long life of nearly ninety years, he remained steadfast and faithful to the Lord Jesus. Not many from his 'caste', who held themselves in lofty isolation had ever turned to Christ in those parts.

My late dad himself was given an interview with Sundar Singh. Sensing that this young disciple was no mere eccentric moved by idle curiosity, Sundar Singh invited him to stay and eat with him in the next place to which he was going. Thus he accompanied Sundar Singh and lived with him for a while, though he very firmly and politely declined the invitation to dine with him, simply because he felt that he was not worthy to sit at the same table with Sundar Singh.

When my dad told Sundar Singh of his longing to go to Tibet with him and to become a martyr for Christ, this man of God clearly indicated to my dad that God would not have him go to Tibet together with him. It was my father's longing as a young man to become a martyr for Christ. As, in Tibet, preaching the Gospel carried the death penalty, that was where my dad wished to go and preach. Furthermore, Sundar Singh emphatically told him that it was a far more important and difficult thing to live a consistent and holy life for Jesus, than to die as a martyr for Christ in remote Tibet. Thus as a young man he was given to understand by Sundar Singh, that God was going to use him mightily amongst young people. Thus my father continued his education and won souls all along the way.

Meeting Sundar Singh or hearing him speak of Jesus, made the whole Gospel narrative come alive in a striking and incontrovertible manner to many in several parts of the globe. My dad and others known to me were amongst those who were deeply influenced by Sundar Singh's life.

My mother too as a young woman heard Sundar Singh and was deeply moved by his preaching.

2

Sundar's Home

The great potentiality of a family no one knows except the One who created the home. God has ordained that men should be the most helpless and innocent creatures at the time of birth. They are placed in the hands of parents and set amidst uncles and aunts, older siblings and cousins.

When God instructed the Israelites through Moses, He emphasized home-training and commanded that children must be taught His precepts while "sitting, standing, walking and lying" and that these precepts must be written on the walls and in places where children would read and learn them. This fervour for teaching children right from their cradle is seen in many orthodox Indian homes. This would be true of quite a high percentage of Hindu, Sikh, Zoroastrian, Buddhist and Moslem families.

Of course, in many nations devout mothers taught their children, even before they went to school, many things of God, according to their understanding. Many great men of God or missionaries came from great mothers who had deep faith in God. Susanna Wesley, the mother of John Wesley, is a striking example of a godly mother who raised great sons.

The mother of Sundar Singh was yet another prototype of a great mother. She did not know about Christ but believed in her own religion. Though she was wealthy, her mind was set on higher things and she wanted her youngest son to be a sadhu—a man wholly devoted to God. His mother told him, "You must not be worldly like your brothers but you must seek 'shanti' (peace and satisfaction in God) which comes from God." She took him to great sadhus and religious leaders and made him hear their words. Even at the age of seven he knew Bhagavadgita* by heart in Sanskrit and began to pore over Hindu religious books while still very young. At the age of twelve he had advanced quite a bit in yoga and studied well all the Vedas and knew some of them by heart. His father was a rich landlord with much money in the bank

*The sacred book of Hindus

14

and gave Sundar all the comforts that he needed.

Their hometown Rampur, in Patiala, is very hot during summer and so they used to retire to the cool heights of Simla, in the Himalayas.

Sundar's period of education in the neighbouring American Presbyterian School was not happy or peaceful at all. The Bible teaching given in the school made him very restless and unhappy. He found the New Testament to be very unlike his religion's Granth which is the holy book of the Sikhs, the other Hindu sacred books, and the Koran of the Mohammedans. He used to interrupt the Scripture classes in the school with many naughty questions and cause as much disruption as possible, when the Bible was taught. The future saint in the making was—both at school and at home—a turbulent boy, leading a gang of youngsters against the preaching of Christ, in his village and neighbourhood.

The pocket money given by his father was used for buying portions of the Bible and making a bonfire of them. One of his early goals was to destroy Christianity. When the shadow of a missionary fell upon him once, he thought he could not be free from the awful pollution which that entailed, until he had washed himself by a prolonged bath of one hour. When Christian preachers were preaching in his neighbourhood or town, he would send his servants to throw cowdung at them.

At the age of thirteen he lost his dear mother. Thus he lost a loving companion and a gentle guide in his life. He had a deep affection for her and her sudden death had a traumatic effect upon him. His life and home appeared to be desolated. Even in the maturity of his later life, he would speak with touching tenderness of his mother. She appears to have given him a very definite direction in his life. Shortly after his mother's death, he stopped going to Christian institutions to study.

3

His Eyes of Understanding Opened

Yoga and concentration (samadhi) have given the sadhus, sanyasis, and the poets of India great mental development and power. These psychic exercises lead to self-hypnotism and also a good deal of self-deception. This in turn creates in them an illusory satisfaction which comes from self-denial and a self-imposed rigorous discipline of both the body and the mind.

So far, I have never met a sadhu or a religious man who could say he had truly found 'shanti' (peace) or God. All they venture to say is that they are still seeking. How can they who reject the only Saviour, who gave His life for the salvation of mankind, get 'shanti' and salvation?

Some of these men, however, can also work

miracles and signs, which totally captivate people. We know that the magicians of Egypt did some of the miracles which Moses performed under the direction of God. Some, by worshipping evil spirits, can do certain things which appear like miracles. Some, by living a life of self-denial and by yogic exercises, can even heal the sick or read others' minds and sometimes even make a clever guess at what the future holds. Many who worship evil spirits can tell the past events of men. Most people do not know that there are powers of darkness, which, if worshipped, can help them on a short-term basis, to feel fulfilled and even be apparently successful. But a true change of character and a new life of holiness, none of these spirits of the underworld can give.

Indian religions are highly developed intellectual achievements of men. The mind, when highly developed, can function in an extraordinary way and even subdue man's instincts and desires. This ultimately results in killing oneself and destroying one's spiritual potentialities. Unlike this, when a man comes under the influence of the Holy Spirit of God, those instincts are not killed but controlled and sanctified and led in the right channels of service. Love with heart purity, love with holiness of life, and faith with humility, which the Lord Jesus gives a repentant sinner, result in a great capacity to bring men under the influence of the Cross of Christ. When people are truly broken at the Cross, the resurrection power of Christ begins to operate in them.

No great Indian sadhu can say, "I can bring salvation to another." The religions of India in their highest disciplines can only bring about a kind of negative ordering of the soul and body, which renders the body as a corpse, while all the time the spirit still remains unkindled and dead. Christ brings salvation to the spirit, soul and body and causes a person to live on a high level of faith, which in turn makes one go and rescue the fallen, and lift them into the New Life and the cleansed walk.

With the passing away of his mother and the deep void it left in Sundar Singh's heart, there came a desperate longing for reality and peace. If ever a man could have found true release and fulfilment through Yoga, it was Sundar Singh, as he was in dead earnest to practise and implement all that this system taught, with all its basic occult overtones. But at this stage, he knew that he had tried all the available methods and meditations known to him, but the deep void persisted.

Earlier, his mother having already taught him a great deal from Hindu Scriptures, had put him under the tutelage of a Hindu pandit and an old Sikh sadhu. But Sundar was bitterly disappointed that they could not show him the secret which would meet his deep inner cravings. Of this period of his life Sundar Singh said, "They taught me with great sympathy and freely gave me the benefit of their experiences, but they had not themselves had that real blessing for which my soul was craving, so how could they help me to get it?"

Sundar's struggles therefore continued. A great sadhu visited their home six months before his conversion and said, "This lad would become in future a great man in the world or a mad person." One day his father rebuked him when he saw him pouring kerosene and burning the Bible with perverse delight. Although he counted it to be a meritorious act, a deep unrest took hold of him shortly after this outburst of bigotry. He could not eat nor sleep for three days. This intense search for finding reality in

God could not go on forever. He wanted to end his life if he could not find that real peace, which his mother had asked him to seek.

On the third night he got up at 2 o' clock and had a bath in cold water for one hour. Then he sat in meditation or prayer and said to God, "O God, if there is a God, if You answer me and give me peace before 5 o' clock this morning and appear to me in your true form, I will serve You as a sadhu all my life. If I do not get an answer from You I will end my life by throwing myself on the rails of the railroad behind my house, when the Ludhiana Mail passes in the morning." Sundar meant what he said. He went on praying and meditating and at four he closed his eyes again. At 4.30 when he again opened his eyes he saw a white smoke-like glow in his room. For a moment he wondered if there was fire in his room. But then came the thought that God perhaps was answering him and he closed his eyes again. As he prayed on, lo, before him stood a glorious figure with such brightness that exceeded the sunshine at midday. Yet he could see it without being dazzled by the sight. Then he saw the crown of thorns on the head of the figure which stood between the ceiling and the floor. There were wounds in the hands, feet and in the side which were bleeding. Having recognized Him to be Christ, Sundar turned away his face saying within himself, "He is none of the incarnations whom I believe." But then he heard these words, "I am Christ whom you are persecuting. There is salvation only through Me. If you believe Me now, you will be saved. If you don't believe Me you will be damned for ever."

Then flashed into his mind the fact that he had never prayed to Christ but to the universal God, to reveal Himself to him. He had challenged God that if He would appear to him, he would never back out but follow Him. He had never, for even a moment, expected that the answer to his prayer was Christ. How could he now refuse the revelation of the Living God? Immediately he fell on the Feet of the Lord Jesus Christ and worshipped Him. A mighty power like the power of electricity flowed into him and a great peace came upon him. He was so full of joy that he ran to his old father, who was sleeping, and woke him up saying that he had seen Christ and that he had given himself to Him. The father remembered the statement of that great sadhu who prophesied that this lad would become either a mad man or a great person. He told his son that something had gone wrong with his mind and that he should go and sleep. In this manner the Lord God Almighty captured for Himself a well-prepared young man to be His follower.

4

Understanding Sundar Singh

In India there are three types of converts: physical, intellectual and spiritual. Some people, when they nominally turn to Christianity, remove all the physical marks and symbols of their earlier religious affiliation, and thereafter begin to attend church services from time to time. Some of the civilising effects of Christian teaching and schools were visibly seen amongst tribal people and those in the lower rungs of the social ladder, particularly in the days of the British Raj*.

The second variety of converts are those who are intellectually convinced and have therefore accepted Jesus Christ with some sacrifice. Amazingly, some of these men later proved to have had subconsciously monetary

*British rule in India ceased on August 15, 1947.

gain in mind too, when they changed their religion. Generally many of these intellectual converts were very learned men, who notwithstanding, had never experienced the power of Christ. In apostle Paul's second letter to Timothy (chp. 3:5 & 7), Paul speaks of men who "have a form of godliness, but deny the power thereof: . . . ever learning, and never able to come to the knowledge of the truth." This is that unspiritual Christianity which has the form but not the power. They appear to learn but never come to comprehend the truth in their hearts. My dad adds: "In fact, I found most leaders of the Indian Church to belong to this category whether they were from the East or West. That is why the Hindu finds very little difference between the psychic and soulish powers of his religion and Christianity."

The people who developed their psychic powers, such as the great sages, sadhus*, poets, and learned men of India, developed the character which St. Paul calls "the righteousness of the law". Several Christian leaders who are intellectuals also have the righteousness of the

---

*Those religious men who have chosen to remain single, in order to give themselves wholly to the pursuit of God.

law, which Saul of Tarsus had before his conversion. Christianity, when it reneges before the onslaught of materialism and 'modern' theology, becomes 'intellectual' and thenceforward has a mere 'form' of righteousness only. A person with that kind of lifeless religion, still maintains polished manners, an even temper, and a certain amount of zeal for God. But this is not the religion which flows from the cross and the broken spirit which one obtains at the nail-pierced Feet of Jesus. The resurrection power of Jesus does not come into play in an intellectual convert's life. Christianity which is not spiritual, does not give its adherents, the experience of the righteousness of God in their hearts. Good training and a disciplined church life, have ofttimes given many people a higher standard of righteousness and morality, as compared to the generality of people. Yet this is not of the Spirit of God. Perhaps back in history, some of these churches too originated out of true Christian roots and revival. Such people as these, have retained a semblance of the discipline and lost the Spirit. With the loss of the Spirit, it is merely a matter of time before the discipline too breaks down.

Thirdly, there are men and women who are

converted from above by the Spirit of God. Now Sundar Singh was one of these. He maintained his spiritual life in Christ because he was not motivated by desire for money or position, nor did he seek the honours which men bestow. He sought to serve his Master in unknown and remote regions, unseen and unapplauded by men. God though, in order to help the Indian and the worldwide Church, brought him into the limelight. This greatly helped to resuscitate a lifeless Church greatly weakened by modernistic unbelief from the turn of the 20th century. Through the impact of this one personality, who was so very like Christ Himself, many were renewed in their faith.

Many leaders and early converts in the Indian Church, who had had remarkable conversion experiences like him, had sunk into shallowness owing to the lure of position and honour, and were lost in polemics, party-strife and controversies. The people who had thus been deflected towards the end of their lives, had lost whatever grip they once had upon God. Sadhu Sundar Singh kept himself away from all such digressions and distractions and served as a 'universal' Christian who faithfully showed forth Jesus, whom Peter and Paul had preached.

It is very unfortunate that in India men who aspire to leadership in the churches, are more anxious to go to colleges in the West for theological training, in order to earn a position and name upon their return, than they are to go to the Word of God, on their knees, before the Living Spirit, who teaches us the Word according to the mind of God. Many promising converts have thus fallen a prey to worldly ambitions and have become a hindrance rather than a blessing to churches. Sundar Singh was never stained by any worldly ambition or love of name or fame. All the acclaim and renown that came to him so early in his life, did not turn him one bit from the simplicity of the Gospel.

My dad used to narrate an incident: "Once on a train I introduced Sundar Singh to a missionary friend of mine. This missionary who was from overseas, immediately joined us in our compartment and began to praise him for his great achievements in his Christian life. Immediately, Sundar Singh showing him his hands, said 'These hands have burnt the Bible. I am a great sinner.'" His tone and the spirit in which he said these words would have silenced any man from further curiosity or flattery. Thus he would turn all the attention upon the great

Saviour who had saved him.

Sundar Singh's sermons were punctuated by his striking personal experiences but they always redounded to the utter glory of his Saviour, Lord and Master. Would to God we could have more men like him who would show the people of today the unparalleled glory of the Christlike life and the abounding power of true discipleship.

5

Living with Sundar Singh

There were too many who were drawn by mere enthusiasm or curiosity and by the renown of Sundar Singh, to peer closely at him or to seek interviews with him. Sundar Singh needed privacy and guarded it very carefully. He preferred not to speak more than twice a day, and used his time for long periods of prayer and communion with God.

Earlier Sundar Singh had been told by his interpreter that young Daniel was not one of those autograph hunters or idly curious persons. Thus Sundar Singh admitted him into close intimacy with himself. Just being with Sundar Singh was an education in itself.

Sundar Singh was very clean in his outward person. Young Daniel could scarcely tell when Sundar Singh managed to wash and dry his one saffron robe, if it were not in the middle of the night. He carried no earthly possessions with him, for he had none. His Bible and his shawl or light blanket, which he draped around his shoulders, were his only possessions. No one could persuade him to carry anything else, not even a small sandwich bag. As for money, he carried none. These impressions etched themselves indelibly in my late father's life, and he himself began to pursue a life of great austerity and simplicity. This was a great help to him in his quest to be Christlike. But that is another story.

These beautiful days of communing with God's servant and watching closely his walk with God came speedily to a close. Either due to his commitments as a student, or through lack of finance to go further with Sundar Singh on his journeys, young Daniel parted with him after the meetings which Sundar Singh addressed at Visakhapatnam. Today, Visakhapatnam is an important naval base and port city on the eastern seaboard of India. Great congregations heard Sundar Singh in the towns of coastal Andhra Pradesh. Now eighty years after those wonderful days of rapturous enthusiasm, no significant stream of lasting value can be traced. Many did dedicate themselves to the Lord Jesus during that time. But in most of their lives the glow and the thrill seemed to have disappeared fast.

The prayer life of Sundar Singh and his Christlikeness had a profound effect on my dad. In his case, deeper longings for higher things and a closer walk with God ensued. Being only a very young school girl then, my mother too was greatly stirred by Sundar Singh. She recalls that together with a host of others, she too made a rather emotional decision to follow Christ. But sadly she too did not perceive any lasting change in her heart and life.

When parting with young Daniel, Sundar Singh gifted to him his shawl, saying that he was giving it to him as a token of his love. The Biblical parallel of the prophet Elijah's mantle falling on young Elisha being unmistakable, many said in fun, "The mantle of Sundar Singh has fallen on Daniel."

When young Daniel returned to his hometown after his sojourn with Sundar Singh, he found his only surviving brother to be critically ill with double-pneumonia. The doctor had abandoned all hope of saving his life, and in those days before antibiotics, there was little hope for one who was so gravely ill with deep-seated infection in the lungs. Overcome by grief, the family withdrew from the bedside of the dying patient and were quietly weeping in the porch. At this juncture, young Daniel, who had arrived on the scene full of renewed faith, walked into the chamber where his brother lay dying, knelt down and spread the blanket of Sundar Singh over him and prayed. Most miraculously, the patient's condition improved. From this point, the change was so marked that people took note that like the aprons which were taken from St. Paul's body brought healing to the sick, the blanket of Sundar Singh had been used of God, to bring about miraculous healing to the dying man.

One would have thought that that blanket would have been preserved as a family heirloom and as an object of awesome veneration, but my father could never say what he managed to do with it, or where he had lost track of it. Fortunately it was the Christ of Sundar Singh whom he followed, and all glory was given to Jesus for this marvellous deliverance.

It must be observed at this point that Sundar

Singh himself became more and more alarmed at the attention he was receiving by the stories of healing which were spreading around him. Further on in his life, he totally declined to do any more healing ministry. Sundar Singh did not want to do anything that appeared to deflect the glory from the Lord Jesus Christ Himself. So in his later years, he refrained from praying for the sick in public. He hated the adulation which was being given to him.

The healing ministry has some peculiar dangers and drawbacks. The people spread the word of the healing they have received and all eyes are soon focused on the human instrument whom the Lord had chosen to use. Often this kind of publicity and praise does little good to young and immature converts, who plunge into the healing ministry without a deep prayer life.

Many from non-Christian backgrounds quickly invest the one who heals in Jesus' Name, with deity and acclaim him as some 'great one'. While the 'gurus' of other religions appear to revel and even cash-in on this adulation, true children of God never cease to be appalled and even greatly revolted by any praise being given to them. Those who do not win this victory over pride and self-glory, will soon find themselves declining spiritually.

6

Expulsion from Home

It was the year 1903, and December with its biting cold was beginning its dreary siege of the Northern plains of India. It was on the third of December that the Lord Jesus appeared to Sundar Singh, just a little while before the suicide which he had planned.

Right from the start, Sundar Singh made no secret of his conversion to Christ. As he publicly began to acknowledge Jesus as his Lord, the rage of his family and relatives waxed even hotter. The example of his own mother, who had sought truth in several religions, was cited by those who sought to dissuade him. Why bring shame upon the whole family and its fair name by following the religion of the foreigner, was the big question which was posed to the young convert. To this day, most Indians make the horrible blunder of thinking that every white person is a Christian. Somehow in their minds, a white skin associates a person with Christianity and thus with a much despised culture. This lends itself, of course, to a great deal of confusion. "How can the religion of drunken revellers and immoral persons do any good to us?" is the common argument in the minds of most people in the East. Most of the people from the West, whom Indians have occasion to meet in travel or professional life, fit this description. Then again they have no notion, that many in Europe and America have no religion at all, and most others merely lend lip service to the traditional dogmas at their churches.

The boy who had hated and ridiculed his Christian teachers, now befriended them to the astonishment of everybody. His erstwhile friends whom he had led in many riotous acts of persecution of Christians, now quickly turned to be his enemies.

Soon the rage of the whole community turned upon the small group of Christians at Rampur. It was organized ostracism. No one would buy from them or sell anything to them. Unable to bear this persecution and threats to their lives and property, most of them fled to a neighbouring place where there was a stronger and older Christian work.

Incidents such as this are quite common in several parts of India. On the conversion of a loved one to Christ, the proverbial tolerance of the 'Hindu' or those of other religions appears to turn into implacable hatred and rancour! Sometimes relatives take an oath to kill a 'new' convert, rather than let him live as a Christian. This underscores the strength and the sinister stranglehold which the caste system has on whole communities.

At this juncture, Sundar Singh persuaded his father to send him to a Christian boys' boarding school in Ludhiana, which was not too far away. The home letters from his father were full of entreaties, pleading with him to renounce his faith in Christ. Every ploy and ruse was employed to wean Sundar away from Christ. His father practically commanded him to get married. That girls can nearly always be depended upon to turn away the heart of a boy, from pursuing God with all his heart, is, of course, common knowledge. If he should get engaged to one in their wider family circles, his father promised him much wealth. But offers of wealth and money had little appeal for Sundar

Singh; his heart was set upon following Jesus.

Finally, when his father ordered him home, he did return to Rampur. But he made it clear to his father, that it was the unchristian lives of the 'Christian' boys at the boarding school which had greatly disappointed him and caused him to return home.

His relatives courted him, "Why should you not marry one of our daughters?" One of them, in fact, showed him a whole chest of gold and golden jewelry and then promised to give it all to him, together with his daughter in marriage. Such are the blandishments with which most Indian boys are enticed by their relatives. But those truly transformed by the Spirit of God are able to withstand all such seductions and pleas, and in many cases press on to do God's will in marriage, thus making a final break with caste.

The ploy used by Sundar Singh's relatives is widely used to this day, in worldly circles. A rich girl is produced; her qualifications and attainments are eulogized; and most of all, the wealth and the lands which are tagged on to the contract, sway the mind of the eligible young man, who in fact had been shopping around.

This is also a device to keep the wealth and property within the family circle, and thus contribute indirectly to the clout of the caste. Thus when a marriage is celebrated in a wealthy Indian home, one can never really tell whether the boy has married the girl or the dowry! After the marriage, great pains are taken to maintain appearances that the couple are a happy pair.

On seeing the fabulous wealth which was offered to him, young Sundar Singh exclaimed, "All this gold cannot give me the peace which the Lord Jesus Christ has given me." The unshakable determination of Sundar Singh to follow Jesus, only made his father more desperate and angry.

But as long as the religious marks sacred to Sikhism were still upon his person, it was felt that there was still some hope of drawing him back to the fold. The long hair, uncut from his childhood, and the bracelet on his hand, were marks that identified him anywhere as a member of the Sikh faith. When young Sundar Singh was constantly being scorned and reprimanded as a renegade and a disgrace to his race, he decided to cut off his long hair. This immediately betokened that his desire to be a disciple of Jesus and renounce Sikhism was decisive. This further infuriated his father.

It was by no means Sundar Singh's intention to aggravate his father, nor was he trying to make a great display of his religious zeal; yet the time had come for him to signify to his family that his discipleship to the Lord Jesus was irrevocable. These were, of course, inevitable steps which one has to take to this day, in one way or another, to free oneself from the age-old tentacles of a strong caste-bound community. His father, no doubt, felt that he could not maintain his standing amidst his people, without forthwith disowning his dear boy.

Thrust out from home, as Sundar Singh walked away into the cold night, with just the clothing which was upon him and his New Testament, he did not know that together with his last meal at home, he had been administered poison which was designed to kill him.

He shivered through the night in the inhospitable jungle and proceeded along the tracks of the railway and caught a train at a station. On the train, he grew gravely ill, vomiting blood. Detraining, he managed to reach the one place in the neighbourhood where loving hands would nurse him back to health from the near-fatal effects of the poison.

The doctor, who was summoned, declared that he would die and was afraid to give any medication whatever, seeing that death was imminent.

When Sundar Singh regained consciousness he told the doctor to read the 16th chapter of the Book of Mark, from the Bible. Narrating this incident much later, Sundar Singh said, "He began to laugh at the story of the Resurrection. In the morning I felt quite fresh and received new life. The doctor came and when he saw me sitting in the sun he was very surprised and felt ashamed and went away without saying a word.

"Some years later when visiting Burma, I met him at a meeting. 'Do you recognise me?' he asked. 'Yes,' I answered, 'I last saw you when on my death-bed.' He told me that my miraculous recovery had made such an impression on him, that he began to read the Bible and was a Christian."

Soon after his recovery, he was received by

two missionaries at Ludhiana. As it happened in scores of other places in India, so here also, mobs threatened to tear down the mission building. His father with tender entreaties made one last attempt to reclaim his boy to his community and tight-knit family.

It is hard for people who have not grown up in the East to understand what a Chinese Buddhist family or a Moslem family as well as a Hindu caste family goes through, when a son or a daughter turns to the Lord Jesus Christ. It is painful to realize, that this fanatic zeal to so seal the caste circle as to preclude the possibility of a break-away, has nothing at all to do with uprightness of life or purity of heart. The factor so vital to conversion—which is turning away from all unrighteousness and evil in one's life— is something which amazingly does not figure at all in the thinking of those who are hostile to the spread of Christianity in India.

When one pleads with the family and says, "But you know very well that your son is free from his drug-addiction today because of Jesus," or "Your husband has become a faithful husband after long years of immorality by being changed by the Lord Jesus," it simply has no weight with them. It is as though they would say, "We would rather have him as an alcoholic or drug-addict but not as a Christian!" One mother actually said recently that she would rather have her son visit prostitutes than turn to Jesus!

This practically fanatic adherence to an inherited way of life, which is essentially based on ignorance, greed, mistrust of others and an intolerance of anything which is not native to their insular culture, is a serious road-block to all progress. This inflexible attitude in the vast majority of people makes a mockery of secularism in government, and even the talk of national integration at a country-wide level is simply unworkable. The dividing walls of caste and lovelessness must first be broken.

What a deliverance the Cross of Jesus brings, which causes an individual to love and labour for everybody around him, setting him free from the blind age-old fears and superstitions and the congenital mental block of caste. The love of the Cross cut through all the shackles for Sundar Singh. From thenceforth Sundar Singh was free to love and serve all men—white, brown, black, or yellow. Wherever he went he won a place in people's love and esteem.

Sundar Singh was waiting for his sixteenth birthday. It was not right that anyone should be legally implicated with respect to his conversion.* If he were baptized after he was sixteen, as the law stood at that time, he and he alone would be held responsible for his choice to follow Jesus. Thus on September the third—his sixteenth birthday—he was baptized by Rev. G. Redman and Canon Chandu Lal at Christ Church, Simla, in the lower ranges of the Himalayas.

Shimla, as Simla is now called, is the capital of Himachal Pradesh (Himalayan State). For scenic beauty, it rivals the Kashmir valley. Through quite a bit of his short life, Sundar Singh used the solitude of the lovely heights of this Himalayan region for prayer, meditation and recuperation from his long evangelistic journeys.

*Although no pressure of any sort was brought to bear upon young Sundar, those around him had to guard against false charges being brought against them. It is very common for people in India to assume that some monetary marriage inducements have occasioned the 'conversion'. That Christ had brought into that person a glorious change of heart and a marvellous sense of peace and present salvation nowhere figures in their thinking.

7

Strangeness of the Cluttered Christian Scene

Sad to say, a genuine convert like Sundar Singh was rare to come by in many districts and towns of India. Every conversion to Christianity ought indeed to be a supernatural event, anywhere in the world. No one is ever born a Christian, nor do you become one by some religious ceremony or by long adherence to hoary tradition. When you really reach out with a broken spirit and touch the Lord Jesus, then you are made whole and you are born-again.

Divinely appointed agents can point you to repentance, but the actual spiritual rebirth itself is by the Spirit of God. By rebirth we mean a total inner transformation, when your sins are washed in the Blood of Jesus. This experience is accompanied by a great peace flooding the soul. This reference to rebirth is not to be confused with the vain and foolish theory of the 'cycle of births', otherwise called the transmigration of souls.

In a country cluttered by a wide range of organizations, some genuinely moved by the desire to lift and save men from spiritual darkness, depravity and suffering, and others, with no real deep sense of mission but rather committed to the humanistic ideal of social uplift and service, there are bound to be a large number of adherents and hangers-on, who show forth no true marks of spiritual conversion. Sundar Singh, therefore, was almost an oddity amongst such proselytes, produced largely by money from overseas and other self-serving considerations. These nominal Christians first viewed him with awe and venerated him. Soon they turned away from him and dismissed him as an over-enthusiastic, over zealous upstart and even as a 'rival' for the missionaries' favours. It came as a shock to him when he met this mass of unspiritual Christians.

Some discerning missionaries from abroad, however, befriended this young convert. But he was shy and uneasy in their company, until a true kinship in spirit was discovered. But those good men who befriended Sunder Singh at this stage were godly, dedicated and well-meaning men, who wanted to shelter the young disciple from the numerous dangers which a new convert faces.

Not very long after his baptism, Sundar Singh set out on a long missionary journey preaching Christ to all who would hear him. His youthfulness and yellow robe immediately gained attention and opened many doors for him. The saffron robe being the hall-mark of Hindu sadhus and sanyasis, he would be taken initially for a Hindu devotee of some standing. But when he proclaimed Christ, the initial interest would turn into surprise, then resentment and finally opposition to his preaching. From village to village he went, sometimes his feet bleeding from the cuts and bruises sustained on the rough Indian roads and bullock cart tracks. He had, however, no baggage to carry; his only possessions being his Bible and his thin shawl which he draped around his shoulders.

Unlike most of us who would hate to venture into the place from which we were turned out in apparent disgrace, Sundar Singh retraced his steps to his hometown of Rampur, in order to proclaim the Good News in Christ. To his surprise, many heard him gladly. The tradesmen were also friendly. Many avenues to preach Christ were opened to him which were formerly totally inaccessible to the Gospel. He was able to enter many well-to-do homes and proclaim Jesus to women, who would normally disdain all social contact with Christians, whom they deemed to be too low in the caste ladder to even admit into their dwelling places.

At his own home, when he knocked, his dad would scarcely admit him. But then he relented and said: "Very well, you can stay here tonight, but you must get out early in the morning and not show me your face again." Sundar wrote in his diary that that night his dad made him sit at a distance that he may not pollute the inmates of the house or the vessels and gave him food. He wrote, "He gave me water to drink by pouring it into my hands from a vessel held high above, as one does who gives drink to an outcaste. When I (received) saw this treatment I could not restrain the tears flowing from my eyes that my father who used to love me so much, now hated me as if I was an untouchable. In spite of all this, my heart was filled with inexpressible peace, . . . I thanked him and respectfully said, 'good-bye' and went away. In the fields, I prayed and thanked God and then slept under a tree, and in the morning continued on my way."

8

Perilous Journeys and Divine Deliverances

Earnest seeking after 'true peace' or 'shanti' as it is termed in Sanskrit, has a long tradition in India. Men renounced enormous wealth and possessions to retire into remote regions to seek salvation for their souls through meditation. Against this inbred and largely undefinable longing for God amongst the generality of Hindus, Christianity in India at the turn of the 20th century had become so bland and lifeless that it reflected more the ritual and cultural practices of nominal Christians in Europe and America than anything else. Sundar Singh, who saw little of Christ in all these Western traditions, was bewildered and turned off by the mere imitation of Western ways, which he came up with in the mission circles. To him the highly structured and regimented systems which he came up with, appeared alien and restrictive. He did not sense any real desire to be like the Master and Lord. Furthermore, the ideal of a self-denying life, a life moved by the love of Jesus which involved his being continually on the road preaching Christ from place to place, appealed strongly to him.*

Possessed of a burning heart, he was aflame to tell all whom he could reach, of the love of God in Christ Jesus. The image of an ill-kept figure, robed in filthy garments, trudging along the dusty Indian road is the kind of picture that the thought of a 'sadhu' conjures before one's mind. Sundar Singh was distinctly different. His person and attire at all times were clean. My father, during his sojourn with him, was not a little surprised at how clean Sundar Singh managed to keep himself and his sadhu's yellow robe.

Brought up in luxury, but now homeless, he faced the rigours of the severe North-Indian winter with a quiet courage. His journeys took him moreover into the most inhospitable terrain imaginable. Still a tender boy in his teens, he carried the Word of God into some of the most

*Moreover it was akin to a tradition with which he was familiar—the life of a 'sadhu'.

fanatical and isolated strongholds of religious bigotry in the rugged countryside of Baluchistan and Afghanistan. Before the snows closed the passes, he travelled into Kashmir, too.

In one place where no one would receive him, due to their implacable hatred for the Good News in Christ, he had to find shelter in a ruined hut by the roadside. Strangely, he kept warm through the night and did not realize until the morning that his bed fellow was a large cobra which had curled up beside him! In the morning, when he arose and saw the cobra, he instinctively recoiled at the sight of the venomous creature and quickly fled the scene. Everyone who knows anything at all of the cobra, knows that it is not to be trifled with. If it takes the notion it attacks with deadly fury and bites with the speed of lightning. Death comes so swiftly too to those bitten by a cobra that medical help can scarcely reach the patient in time. Then the Lord gently rebuked him saying, "Did I not keep you safe through the night? Go and retrieve your shawl." As he drew his shawl, the snake quietly slithered away.

In one place, he saw a hostile mob advancing menacingly towards him making no effort to hide their intentions to do him bodily harm. Sundar Singh, aware that he could not escape their fury and rage with his life, knelt down and committed his spirit to the Lord, being convinced that his end was near. On rising up from prayer and looking down from the eminence where he was, he saw the mob fleeing in great disorder.

Next day, the same mob appeared in the distance and Sundar Singh felt that they were now advancing upon him with the resolve firmly renewed to dispatch him. By this time, as the crowd drew near, they displayed no malicious intentions. Sundar Singh, however, met them with resignation and told them that he was ready to be killed for Jesus. But they told him what had really happened the previous day. "We indeed came yesterday to kill you; but we saw around you some resplendent beings clad in white. Terror filled our hearts and we fled." Sundar Singh had not realized that the angels of God had come and surrounded him when the mob was drawing near. "Who were those men who surrounded you?" his erstwhile foes asked. Now there was only one answer to this question. "The angel of the Lord encampeth round about them that fear him, and delivereth them" (Psalm

34:7). For, humanly speaking, there was not a single person with him. Then the same crowd that had thirsted for his blood the previous day, heard the Word of the Lord from Sundar Singh's lips with deep godly fear.

When Sundar Singh was still very young and inexperienced, he happened to meet a man of great zeal and devotion by the name of Samuel Stokes. Stokes, who was an American, loved the Indian people so greatly that he appeared to be ready to die for them. In his company, Sundar Singh learnt of others before him, such as St. Francis of Assisi and his disciples, who walked close to Jesus and lived selfless lives of service, moving constantly from place to place.

Patterning his life on that of St. Francis of Assisi, who in all aspects of his life wanted to mirror the life of Jesus, Stokes renounced all his possessions and after giving them away to the needy, hit the road, ministering to the sick and suffering.

With Stokes he travelled several hundred miles by foot. Stokes wrote of Sundar: "His work has been far better than my own, and although he is scarcely more than a boy, he has suffered hunger, cold, sickness and even imprisonment for his Master."

On one occasion, when Sundar Singh was suffering greatly amidst the cold, stricken by malaria, Stokes, being greatly concerned, drew the shawl from Sundar's face to see how he was. Shivering and burning with fever as he was, Sundar with a radiant face was heard saying, "How sweet it is to suffer for Jesus!"

Sundar Singh's zeal for the Lord Jesus and his practice of Christian discipleship comes as a rebuke to the soft, over-cuddled, comfortable Christian believer of today.

One is aghast at the reactions of horror, dismay and insecurity noticeable in those who call themselves Christians, at the approach of the slightest adversity or affliction. "Endure hardness, as a good soldier of Jesus Christ" (2 Timothy 2:3) is all but forgotten! How distressing to see young promising converts to Christ with great potential led forth into the paths of ease and selfishness, by the evil example of older Christians, whose lives have nothing of challenge or example to offer!

The famous C. F. Andrews, the writer, came up with Sundar Singh and Stokes up in the mountains around Simla, at a small place called Kotgarh on the road to Tibet. Mr. Andrews speaks of the fresh-faced boy whom he met thus: "His face had the look of childhood . . . in spite of the marks of pain which were also there. At first sight it was not so much his face that attracted my attention, as his marvellous eyes. They were luminous like the darkly gleaming water of some pool in the forest, which is touched by a ray of sunlight."

C. F. Andrews also wrote: "There was a cave just above the village of Kotgarh. That cave became the home of Sundar Singh and Stokes, and his little band of young lads. They were indeed a very strange company. Two were children of lepers, who were themselves suspected of leprosy; another was blind and one was a cripple. Stokes had fathered and mothered them all, like a hen under his own wing. But a merrier company you would rarely meet in the world. They hardly knew what sorrow was." Living simply and frugally with that little band, Sundar was laying some strong foundations for rigorous labours ahead.

Thus, in encountering the sturdy discipleship of this young disciple Sundar Singh, many will want to dismiss him as some kind of super-disciple who has little to say to them. No! Let us stop and absorb the challenge. We too can allow the Spirit of God to mould our life-style such that we become Christlike in thought and action.

There is a frightening insularity in seemingly good Christian churches and fellowships, where the snare of carving a comfortable niche for one's self amidst pleasant surroundings, is keeping many from great goals.

9

Murderous Bandit Tamed and Other Incidents

The strict chronology of all the incidents and miracles that took place in Sundar Singh's itinerations is hard to determine. But facts are facts and all these exploits of faith bring great stimulus to our souls.

As he trudged along a lonely road in an area particularly notorious for bandits, Sundar Singh was suddenly accosted one day by a bandit accustomed to summarily killing travellers and seizing and plundering their valuables. When Sundar Singh met this cruel man who blocked his path with an upraised sword, he meekly put down his head and expected the sword to fall at any moment. But, to his surprise, the man lowered his sword and his manner changed completely! He could not believe that a man who was strong and tall like Sundar Singh would so meekly submit. Wondering at the words of Sundar Singh he led him to a cave. The bandit took him into the interior of the cave. There in the nether part, Sundar Singh saw the skeletons of men who had been killed by him. The bandit exclaimed, "All these men have I killed! Will God forgive me?" There Sundar Singh proclaimed to this desperate and wicked man the forgiveness which the Lord Jesus offers to sinners.

As he went on his way, Sundar Singh realized with much thankfulness to God that he was spared from death that day and rejoiced that he could point a truly miserable sinner to the Saviour who came to seek and save the lost.

While Sundar Singh moved amongst inhospitable regions and trudged across terrain which few humans crossed, without any question, it was the angel of the Lord who protected and guarded his footsteps, until his work on earth was done.

Those who roomed or lived with him, not only saw but recorded some of the marvellous events which seemed to constantly take place around him. Thus, a gentleman who later became a YMCA secretary in England, wrote of that night which had left him stunned and speechless: "Long after midnight, I was roused by a movement in the room. The Sadhu had risen from his bed and was moving towards the door, which opened on the wooden stairs outside the house. The creaking of the wood made it clear that he was going down. Knowing that the Sadhu spent hours of the night in prayer, I was not surprised at this. But when half an hour or so had passed and he had not returned, I became uneasy; the thought of the leopard in the valley made me feel anxious. So I got out of bed, . . . and looked out of the window towards the forest. A few yards from the house I saw the Sadhu sitting, looking down into the deep valley. It was a beautiful night. The stars were shining brightly . . . For a few moments I watched the silent figure of the Sadhu. Then my eyes were attracted by something moving on his right. An animal was coming towards him. As it got nearer I saw that it was a leopard. Choked with fear, I stood motionless near the window, unable even to call. Just then the Sadhu turned his face towards the animal and held out his hand. As though it had been a dog, the leopard lay down and stretched out its head to be stroked.

"It was a strange, unbelievable scene, and I can never forget it. A short time afterwards the Sadhu returned and was soon asleep but I lay awake wondering . . ."

The foregoing deliverance brings to mind the more famous incident when a man-eating wolf was rebuked and tamed by St. Francis of Assisi. Incredible as it might seem, people who walk close to Jesus Christ have exercised this strange power both over blood-thirsty bandits and cruel beasts of prey.

The present writer knows of other incidents where tigers came to within two or three metres of our men who had retired for solitary prayer in areas which are frequented by wild animals, yet would not harm them.*

*The present author, who leads the Laymen's Evangelical Fellowship International, can speak of stations and our workers who labour where wild elephants, bison and tigers roam. Some of our workers, who take the Good News of Jesus Christ to these jungles where tribal people live, hazard their lives week after week. God in His mercy has kept numerous of our workers and their children, from these animals which regularly kill human beings who cross their path, and also from huge snakes whose bite is fatal.

On one of his journeys, Sundar encountered a pathetic sight, where a man stood mourning and grieving over the death of a companion. The story of this mourner was that he and his friend were travelling, when his companion suddenly took ill, collapsed and died. There lay the body covered by a shroud by the roadside. The narrator of this sad story went on to say that he was absolutely penniless and had no money with which to cremate or otherwise arrange for the removal of his companion's body.

Sundar Singh was moved by pity, and although he had so little and carried hardly any money, he tried to do for this man what he could by way of relieving his distress. He had not proceeded far from the sad scene, when Sundar Singh heard even yet louder and more frantic wails. The man whom he had just tried to comfort and relieve came running to him saying, "My friend has really died!" Then it was that Sundar Singh came to realize that these were two conmen who employed this ploy to obtain alms and gifts from the travellers who passed by.

After receiving help from Sundar Singh, this fellow had gone back and called on his friend to rise, but his friend made no response. It was their practice to play the dead man in turns. Once the road was clear, they would be their usual selves again! Now, though the road was clear, he could not rouse his friend who would normally spring back to 'instant health' when called. Now to his real sorrow and distress, he found that his companion was dead. This must have come as a great shock to Sundar Singh himself. No man of God would desire the death even of a deceiver.

While God Himself has no joy in the death of a sinner—Ezekiel 18:32: "I have no pleasure in the death of him that dieth"—yet there is a very particular retribution which is meted out to those who lie, deceive and slander men of God who are key instruments in the building of His work and Kingdom. The present writer himself has seen cases like this, when God used his late father in great revival power, when mighty works of God spontaneously took place and were witnessed by thousands of people. We have seen strong men suddenly fall down and come close to dying, and even expiring suddenly, when they uttered blatant lies where God was at work, i.e., in the midst of a revival environment. Pretence, deception, lies, stealing and adultery, when deliberately hidden in the midst of praying people, carry a very heavy penalty and can be visited with serious judgments from God.

10

The Sadhu Robe—
Saffron Attire

Sundar Singh strongly felt that if Christ was presented to India in terms more native to their thought-patterns and ideas, it would be easier for the people to overcome their prejudice and accept Christ. Hailing as he did from a rural village with all its orthodoxy, prejudice and fanatic adherence to old beliefs and practices, he saw how antagonistic the people were to anything which smacked of the West and an alien culture. There is, no doubt, a great deal of truth in this. Hence he wanted to present Christ to the Indian people with a wrapping which appealed to them.

A strong movement for national independence from British rule was being cranked up at that time, around the early part of the twentieth century. This engendered a violent revulsion of everything British in a particular sense, and foreign in a general sense. The British government, of course, had established chapels and churches at all their cantonments and army garrison towns and seats of government—not out of a missionary love for the local people, or solicitude for their souls, but because they had to provide baptism and burial for their nationals. These churches were merely an extension of the State Church of England, which was regulated by the Ecclesiastical Department which was a department of the Government. The East India Company, which was the precursor of the British Government of India, had definite rules against missionaries coming to India or operating out of areas under British control. They feared that missionaries would be meddlesome and upset the nationals by their teaching. Thus it was that William Carey, the father of modern missions, positioned himself in a Dutch enclave near Calcutta. That Carey and the early missionaries had run the risk of being arrested and repatriated to England, is little known to people today.

It was part of the British protocol of those days that the English Bishop was next only to the Governor. All high-ranking officials of

Government were required to show up at the Sunday Services, a minimum number of times in the year. Of course, these were ordinary men with all the vices which belonged to the ruling classes anywhere in colonial lands. Hence the tragic and totally unwarranted association, which got firmly fixed in the minds of ethnic people all over the world that the white skin is synonymous with a Christian. This false assumption is still dominant in the minds of many and has militated strongly against the Gospel.

Now while the British administrator in India had always been credited with honesty, fairplay, and even-handedness, his character was not necessarily Christian, to say the least.

The elite corps of officers and administrators, who were obliged out of custom or the regulations of Government service to attend the Anglican services, sometimes took great umbrage at the preaching of godly chaplains who would not spare their sins. There were some exceptionally godly men among these Government-appointed clerics, who developed sympathies and concerns far beyond the call of duty and loved the people of India

71

and longed for their salvation.

A few men in the ruling classes were also noteworthy Christian men, who did a great deal of good in the districts where they were either Revenue officials or members of the judiciary. These men sometimes joined hands with the missionaries to help in securing suitable lands for their schools, colleges, hospitals, leprosaria and other needful developmental activities.*

Our readers will better understand now how, fixed in the Indian mind, there has remained this false notion that Christians and the white skin are indissolubly linked together. Hence Christianity, to this day, is always thought of as the religion of the white man. Now, this false premise has been a great stumbling block to many who have never cared to enquire in any depth into this stumbling-block of the ignorant and the immature. Even highly educated people labour under this most foolish of all notions and prejudices. This is, however, strongly indicative

*While outwardly the missionaries were lauded and praised for their noble, self-sacrificing services by the public, yet in reality any little concession or help given by the government to a missionary sponsor of a humanitarian cause was deeply resented.

of the inbuilt bias and antagonism to Christ, which is prevalent in most people of the East. Thinking about it, you must know, as the present writer travels and works with young people of many nations, he meets ofttimes with a stronger indifference and antipathy to Christ in certain regions of the Western hemisphere than anything which he has seen in India.

Now, this was the backdrop against which Sundar Singh began his missionary labours. The tradition of a young man clad in yellow robes who had renounced marriage and was therefore given the honorific 'sadhu', gave a person freedom of travel, as a prerequisite of his calling. Moreover, a sadhu would be accepted in circles where a white-robed or black-robed Christian priest or pastor would be turned away. The people had been taught by long tradition to reverence a person who had made the requisite sacrifices to become a sadhu. Sundar Singh, in donning a yellow robe, immediately made himself accessible to many common people. They felt they could communicate with a man in a yellow robe. There was much which they shared with him in common. There were occasions too when people were moved to the nth degree of rage and violent vituperation and disgust when they discovered that this sadhu was preaching Christ, and not the gods or the ancient epics and Vedas, whom alone they venerated. Thus he was thrust out of villages when it was discovered that he was a Christian. But without question, after all has been said, the sadhu's robe was a great help just to communicate and enter communities where no ordinary Christian preacher could commonly go.

Those eccentric preachers who travel to Western lands and appear on platforms in attire which belongs to their native lands, merely seek to play upon the minds of shallow listeners, who love to see something novel and are drawn to any clownish person who claims to be a 'guru' from the East. Sundar Singh, of course, is not to be classed with any of these clowns. His heart's desire was to communicate Christ, and this he did in a way which few have equalled in history.

Sundar Singh's serene and glowing countenance with its beautifully chiselled features made many people think that he closely resembled the Lord Jesus, even in his external appearance.

11

At St. John's Divinity College

The friends and well-wishers of Sundar Singh wanted to make sure that he was not lost to the Indian Church. Hence they prevailed upon him to join the Divinity College at Lahore, there to receive a theological education which would lead on to ordination and licensing to preach in the Anglican Church.

It must have taken a supreme effort of the will for Sundar Singh to confine himself to the intellectual training of the class room. To one who had practical communion with God and a growing knowledge of God from walking intimately with Him through a life of prayer, some of the lectures on the Book of Common Prayer, History of Religion, Apologetics, etc., were rather insipid and quite academic in content. It was but natural for him to feel strange in the usually unreal atmosphere of the theological college, where semantics is specialized in rather than the practical application of the Scripture.

His classmates too kind of kept him at arm's length from them because he seemed a strange character to them. Probably they had already acquired the regrettable propensity so redolent of theological circles, of holding practical religion in disdain. In any case, Sundar Singh almost felt he was a stranger among them. He managed, however, to complete a few courses and was granted a licence to preach.

The saintly Bishop Lefroy tried to convince Sundar Singh that ordination would mean that he confined his attention to a single parish or to a small group of churches. Sundar Singh himself was burning with a longing to reach the unreached areas with the Gospel and to awaken an unfeeling church which had lost its mission, wherever he found it, from the north to the south in India. The Bishop gently tried to convince him that such itinerations and free-wheeling from diocese to diocese would simply not be possible, as the regulations of the Anglican Church would not permit it. Sundar Singh, of course, felt that on these terms he must refuse ordination and without any hard feelings he also returned the licence to preach in that diocese. Henceforth he belonged to all churches and would preach wherever God took him.

It is hard to imagine how Sundar Singh felt in his heart when the good Bishop tried to convince him that his protracted tours to Tibet would be quite impossible, when he was ordained in the Episcopal Church. Tibet was close to his heart. He felt strongly that whereas missionaries had failed to establish the work of God in Tibet down the centuries, it was the special responsibility of the Indian Church to take Christ to the people of Tibet. That Tibet was still a 'closed' land was not thought of as being of any great consequence by Sundar Singh. Perhaps it can be irrefutably stated that more than any other single person's, Sundar Singh's twenty missionary journeys into Tibet were the most serious onslaughts which were ever launched on the superstitions, fear and degradation in which Tibet lay.

12

The First of His Tibetan Journeys

"In prisons more frequent, in deaths oft"
(2 Corinthians 11:23)

Now that his short stint of eight months at Theological School was finished, Sundar Singh plunged again into the glorious mission of making Christ known to all who would hear. It was in July 1910 that Sundar Singh secured his release from the seminary. His stay there however left some changes in lives, which would last long after he himself ceased from his labours.

Simla, the beautiful hill station much favoured by the British for its invigorating climate and which served as the summer residence of the Viceroys of India, was a kind of gateway for anyone bent on making the hazardous trips to Tibet. It is somewhat incredible to think that in his short life Sundar Singh made no less than twenty trips to Tibet. Everyone of these trips was fraught with innumerable perils and grave dangers to his life. Besides robbers, steep, slippery narrow paths were the least of the dangers. But hardships never worried him.

Looking west from Simla, one had to travel some lonely precipitous roads. Kotgarh was a natural halting place. On the way to Kotgarh, in a tiny village, Sundar Singh came upon reapers busy with their harvest. Being busy with their scythes, they paused to listen to the message of this young sadhu. But, on finding that he preached the Christian message, the owner of the lands and his brother were so incensed at his intrusion that the former hurled a stone at the sadhu. The stone hit Sundar Singh just above the eye and he bled from the wound. Quietly he went to a cold stream close by, bathed his wound and returned to the field. The reapers had observed how he had not cast a spell or even uttered a word of cursing at the man who had caused him injury. They had expected a furious response from the holy man. The reapers, however, were not at all surprised when the stone-thrower was suddenly overwhelmed and sank down with a splitting headache. Sundar quietly took up his scythe and began harvesting the corner of the field, where the stricken man had been working. When the harvest was gathered in, it was observed that that part of the field where Sundar Singh had harvested had yielded in great abundance!

That evening Sundar Singh was received most respectfully in the village and was given total liberty to preach Christ to the people. And whenever he happened to pass by, he was assured of a warm welcome here.

On his first visit to Tibet, Sundar Singh did not penetrate very far into the country, but sufficient to see the abject squalor and degradation in which the people lived. Even to Sundar Singh who was well-used to backward and undeveloped regions, where he had lived and laboured, Tibet was a profound shock. People who deemed a bath to be a sin and whose houses were insanitary and ill-kept hovels and whose minds were fast shut to all enlightenment and change, presented a most difficult and challenging mission field.

When Sundar Singh had his customary bath, the people were practically convinced that he could not be a holy man, since he did such a dreadful thing as taking a bath! Thus he met much hostility everywhere. Only in one place, the head lama welcomed him and permitted him to preach to the monks in his monastery.

The parched and dried barley, which was the only food available, was so hard to chew that Sundar Singh was convinced that even the domestic animals would not touch it! How he survived on such fare, it is quite hard to imagine. Tibetan tea too was equally unappetizing, seeing that it was drunk with salt and a liberal helping of rancid butter.

Anyone passing to Tibet over the high passes of the Himalayas had always to be on his guard to retrace his steps before the heavy snowfalls completely closed the passes. Thus Sundar Singh returned to India across the Himalayas before the passes became impassable but his mind was set upon going back to Tibet in the next summer.

13

More Tibetan Journeys

When God gives a vision to a man it stays. There may be temporary setbacks and delays, but a man who is guided by the Spirit of God will not be deflected even if there is very real danger to his life. Reaching the needy and scattered communities in the wilderness of Tibet's high plateau was a burden laid upon Sundar Singh's heart by God, and he carried out this mission with a passionate zeal to declare Christ, where His saving Name was never heard before.

Nineteen more journeys followed between 1908 and 1929. Kotgarh, at 7000 feet elevation, about fifty miles away from Simla, became a kind of base camp for Sundar Singh for his journeys into Tibet and also as a resting place for prayer, where he refuelled in God's presence.

Even on the borders of Tibet he found

consecrated Moravian missionaries from Germany. The Moravian Church had sent out its missionaries from the beginning of the eighteenth century after they had experienced revival and had established their brotherhood at Herrenhut. Herrenhut is situated deep in the erstwhile communist East Germany and close to the borders of Poland. In the ancient cemetery of this village are the graves of the founders of this movement, Count Zinzendorf and his wife. Young men had moved out of Herrenhut, burning with zeal to carry Christ to the remote corners of the globe. Some of them had left with a mere light bag or two, to traverse the whole land mass of Europe and Asia and to cross the oceans. They did not give in to the dangers which they faced but penetrated even to Kashmir and the borders of Tibet. One of these dedicated men even translated the Bible into Tibetan.

Now Sundar Singh met two of these godly men by the names of Kunick and Marx, doing their work for Christ and reaching souls without publicity and fanfare. The media was not there to trumpet out or photograph the exploits of these two heroes, who had thought nothing of sacrificing so much, to serve people. Some of our modern heroes, who do exploits with the finest of equipment and with the aid of the latest space-age gadgets, are nothing compared to these early heroes of the Cross. The Moravian Mission had three stations at Leh, Keylang and Pooh, respectively. Their chief work was in these places close to Tibet's borders.

Kunick and Marx received Sundar Singh and taught him some elements of the Tibetan language and even gave him an interpreter to help him in his work.

As Sundar Singh ventured deeper into Tibet and explored new routes which were not customarily used by travellers, more of the desperate need of Tibet was unveiled before his eyes. Prayer flags fluttered everywhere from the courtyards of dwellings, as though God needed to be signalled and His attention caught by a flag! Some of these flags, in fact, had become so filthy and tattered from exposure to rain and dust that they made a sad and sickening sight.*

*Even in Trinidad and other regions, where Indians had migrated centuries ago, these flags flutter conspicuously. In India itself, amongst the multitude of idolatrous symbols, you will but very rarely come up with prayer flags.

There were the peasants who carried prayer wheels. A little scroll with some mysterious writing or chant is whirled round and round by the turning of what was called the prayer wheel. Hence by this mechanical motion, one is said to be saying so many prayers.

It is so enigmatic that in neighbouring Nepal, wheels were totally outlawed for centuries. How strange that in that whole region, while they counted upon a wheel to say their prayers for them, it could not be used for mobility on a carriage or cart. It is because the wheel was thought to be totally sinful, that Nepal saw no need to have roads! Even into the middle of the twentieth century, once one got out of Khatmandu, the capital of Nepal, the tracks or paths which pedestrians used for ages, were barely jeepable.

Some of the grosser manifestations of superstition, evidence of which was everywhere present, must have greatly saddened the heart of Sundar Singh, who had found such great release in Christ from the superstitious practices of his own native culture. His own experience that prayer from a broken heart and in the Name of Jesus was effective to achieve impossible things, was so far removed from the practices of these poor people, who were paralyzed by their false religion. He was just at that time of life when one is fired by an unquenchable love for souls and an insatiable desire to do exploits for the Saviour.

In one place the people were so roused with fanatical hatred that they beat him, bound him and dragged him out of the village and left him to die, having put blood-sucking leeches on his body. When consciousness returned, his tortured body ached and he heard the calls of wild animals from the jungle and lapsed back into unconsciousness.

The crowd that had savagely beaten him were convinced that there was no way by which he could survive the night. But when he returned to consciousness again, he found two men gently bathing his wounds. His hands were now free as his bonds had been removed. Where there had been deep wounds he had been bandaged.

Now, who were these men who had taken pity on him to come to his aid in such a remote place? When he was sufficiently recovered, in the dead of night, they gently led him out of the jungle to safety. God had sent two of his disciples, who loved Jesus in spite of all the hatred for Him and the fanatic intolerance prevalent in that area towards Christianity.

These two men whispered to Sundar Singh that they were secret believers in Jesus. To Sundar Singh, and for that matter for any true believer in Jesus, the concept of being a secret believer is totally unthinkable as well as being unscriptural; for Jesus Himself said, "Whosoever shall be ashamed of me and of my words, of him shall the Son of man be ashamed, when he shall come in his own glory, and in his Father's and of the holy angels" (Luke 9:26). Yet to Sundar Singh's great surprise, even from the city of Banares extending to the secluded caves of the Himalayas, he met these men. They claimed to be the members of a society which called itself Secret Sanyasi Mission. In the course of their earnest seeking for the universal God—to their profound shock or surprise—the Lord Jesus revealed Himself to them. In the conversion of some of these men, there was hardly any human agency! Hence it is not surprising that their subsequent history showed quite clearly that they lacked spiritual instruction. No one had taken them in hand as Aquila and Priscilla had received the gifted disciple Apollos at Ephesus 'to expound unto him the way of God more perfectly' (Acts 18:26).

On one occasion, weary and blinded by the snow, when Sundar Singh was painstakingly dragging himself forward over a treacherous mountain, he slipped and fell. How much down the mountain the fall took him is not clear and also how long he lay unconscious is not known. But when he opened his eyes, he saw a most fearful-looking creature, which he could not identify, advancing towards him. He could only imagine that it must be a very aged human being so covered with hair, that he almost appeared like a wild animal. To Sundar Singh's great amazement, this aged person said, "Let us pray!" Then he proceeded to pray in the Name of Jesus. This sage, of whom only a few men were aware, had first come to India and the Himalayas, drawn by a great love and compassion for the people of the subcontinent of India. After Sundar Singh discovered him and revealed the fact to others, the Maharishi became a person who excited much curiosity, enquiry and debate. He was already known to some in the area as the Maharishi of Khailas, which means the great sage of Khailas. Subsequently

Sundar Singh found that wherever he went people would question him about the Maharishi. Quite understandably, after sometime, Sundar Singh became weary of satisfying the curiosity of people concerning the Maharishi, and told them plainly, "I have come to preach Christ, and not the Maharishi."

Here was a man who walked close to God, a true saint and a man who interceded for the nations. His story was breathtaking! Born and brought up as a strict Moslem in the city of Alexandria in the seventeenth century, he joined a Moslem school of priests and trainees, where he studied the Koran, the Moslem's holy book, carefully. He was, however, deeply dissatisfied and felt hungry for the truth, seeing that all his efforts to find God were a failure. How he came upon a saintly missionary from India, by the name of Hieronimus would make another thrilling story I suppose. This Hieronimus was a nephew of that saintly missionary, St. Francis Xavier. The reader must bear in mind that many saintly men of the pre-Reformation and early post-Reformation days were high above man-made dogmas and knew the Saviour and walked with Him. Being with Christ and sitting in His presence, they became what they were—true men of God.

Thus Hieronimus led this struggling seeker to Christ. Those timeless words which Jesus spoke which have drawn men of all ages to Him, "Come unto me, all ye that labour and are heavy laden, and I will give you rest" (Matthew 11:28), and "For God so loved the world, that he gave his only begotten Son, that whosoever believeth in him should not perish, but have everlasting life" (John 3:16), took fast hold of him. He acted on these words and found the glorious release, forgiveness of sins and peace which is commonly known as conversion. Having preached Christ together with his teacher for sometime, he felt a great call to the East.

Most people in India can never realize what feelings of love and compassion surge from the heart of any true disciple of Jesus, who comes to this ancient country for the first time. On coming to India, one surveys the poverty and the oppression, the occult practices and superstitious fears, the hopeless, unbearable grind of the daylong and poorly-rewarded toil which people accept with stoic resignation. All this has the cumulative effect of almost crushing a person of compassion with pangs of love and longing to lift the heavy burden. Thus it was with this missionary who came all the way from Alexandria. Unable to bear the cry and sorrow of the land, he had retired to one of the caves of the Himalayas to plead and pray for the people of this subcontinent and other nations.

Nearly three centuries rolled by while this man of God continued sequestered in the solitude of those remote heights, engaged in the heaviest ministry of all—intercession. He sustained himself by the herbs and the berries of the mountain side. The medicinal quality of some of these herbs had the amazing effect of giving adequate warmth to the body even in the bitter cold of the high altitudes of the Himalayas. This sage introduced Sundar Singh to some of his fare while Sundar Singh tarried with him for some days.

The Maharishi made a point of telling him that he had witnessed the Third Battle of Panipat.

14

Sundar Singh's Evangelistic Journeys

Barely was he out of his twenties before his fame spread everywhere and there were calls to go over and address meetings from widely scattered areas.

As he set out for South India, large crowds greeted him everywhere. In some places they had such a crowded programme scheduled for him, that on arriving he would score out the excessive number of engagements and meetings and choose only to address two important meetings a day. One of these meetings was for missionaries and Christian workers, and in the evening he would address the public meeting.

There was, of course, mounting interest in Sundar Singh as a man. He had a gripping style of speaking and his simple illustrations drawn from everyday life and presentations of the truth were just unforgettable. Citing the Scripture, "For whosoever will save his life shall lose it; but whosoever shall lose his life for my sake and the gospel's, the same shall save it" (Mark 8:35), he had this illustration to give:

On one of his Himalayan journeys in an awful blizzard, he together with another traveller was struggling to reach the next village. It seemed highly improbable that they would make it. In the midst of the storm as they trudged through the deep snow, they saw a man lying apparently dead, by the path. Sundar Singh said to the fellow traveller, "Come, let us carry him to the next village." The traveller was astounded by the proposition and scoffed, "You and I are scarcely likely to save our own lives. It makes no sense to think of carrying a man who is almost dead. I will be no part of your foolishness." So saying, he walked ahead, leaving Sundar Singh with the man who had almost frozen to death. Although he showed few signs of life, it was against the grain for Sundar Singh to leave a dying man to perish in the snow storm. He hoisted the limp figure onto his back and wearily and painstakingly trudged through the snows, step by step. The labour and friction involved when carrying a deadweight, such as a man who was almost lifeless, was perhaps the cause for Sundar's own survival in that dreadful storm. A little while after, Sundar came upon the form of his erstwhile travel companion lying dead in the snow! The cold had killed him. He had tried to save his own life but had lost it. Sundar Singh, by undertaking an impossible task, which on the surface meant certain death for himself, saved his own life. The strenuous exertion involved saved Sundar Singh's life. By the time he reached the next village, the man on his back revived and thus his life was saved too. Illustrations such as this brought the Scriptures vividly alive to Sundar Singh's audiences.

Some in Europe, who had seen Sundar Singh while they were very young, spoke to the present writer of the unforgettable experience.

Sundar Singh, when confronted by the large crowds of nominal Christians in South India, said, "Although there are so many Christians here in the South-western corner of India (now called Kerala), and in the Southern region (now called Tamil Nadu), all forward movement of the church is paralyzed. You are like the legs and feet of India, but you are like feet that are stricken by elephantiasis.* You can't move forward." Now he identified the elephantiasis in the two feet as an adherence to caste on the one hand and dowry on the other. The prevalence of both these abominations within so many churches and the continuing greed of bridegrooms and their parents who demand large amounts of money or gold from the parents of the hapless brides, have stalled all spiritual progress. Thus while many in his great audiences thrilled to his message and apparently responded to his challenge, the lasting or largescale results were but few in South India. Many lapsed back into their somnolence, after the first glow of making a decision at Sundar's meetings. There was not much life in most churches to sustain them in their spiritual life.

There were those, however, who, around the world, were blessed permanently. One young man studying at Oxford sought Sundar Singh's company and became one of the early biographers of Sundar Singh. This present writer met this gentleman when, as the Bishop of Coimbatore Diocese, he attended some of the

*A disease which gathers excess flesh around the feet and upto the knees, such that the feet get so huge and take on the appearance of an elephant's.

revival meetings addressed by him and his late father. Sundar Singh left a deep impression on this erudite bishop. When he took up this bishopric in the Church of South India, there was so much turbulence, warring factions, court cases and rebellion in so many of his churches that the Bishop, seeing no way by which to reach his people, called on the diocese to pray for revival. One of the noteworthy developments which arose out of this call for prayer was that the late father of this present writer was called to address revival meetings in one of the key churches, where Christian work was nearly paralyzed by factionalism and plain wickedness. God, in His infinite mercy, granted a great revival to ensue from these meetings. Thousands were swept into God's kingdom; peace and a period of evangelism and spiritual advance followed. But this is another story.*

It was very striking that the above mentioned Bishop, Bishop Appasamy, when an old man, would slip into the congregation and sit humbly in the pew when the present writer, who was young enough to be his grandson, was in the pulpit preaching. Hence his having sought

*The story of this revival at Erode can be read in the author's book, "Another Daniel".

out Sundar Singh and kept company with him to the extent possible, being a busy scholar at Oxford, did leave a lasting impression and fruit in Bishop Appasamy's life.

The coming of Sundar Singh administered a great shock to sluggish and sleeping churches everywhere.

15

Tibetan Journeys Continued

Inasmuch as Sundar Singh made no less than twenty trips to Tibet, there were incidents galore, fraught with danger and replete with divine interventions. How one would wish to have had a full record of all these Himalayan hazards which were overcome through faith in the Name of Jesus! Even the meagre accounts of the marvellous deliverances with which God manifested His might are a real shot in the arm for many of us who are sadly in danger of becoming chocolate soldiers! Yet, alas, some of these tremendous assays into the realms of darkness and the fruit thereof are lost to us, inasmuch as Sundar Singh himself never recorded them in the midst of the unremitting fury of the battle.

In one Tibetan town by the name of Razar,

his hearers were filled with an overwhelming rage so that Sundar Singh was summarily condemned to die. A cruel method of execution which involved excruciating pain in the midst of a pitiless milieu, was devised by the Buddhist lamas who professed not to be violent. To this extent, however, they were consistent, that they did not quite witness the long-drawn-out and painful death of the condemned. This barbaric measure of torture and death involved that the condemned person was thrown into a deep well, where the rotting and decomposed bodies of those who had been condemned earlier lay strewn all around him at the bottom of the well. The fall itself entailed serious injury when thrown down from the top. Secondly, there was the unbearable stench of decomposing corpses, and the condemned man died a slow and painful death in the midst of these gruesome surroundings. Now Sundar Singh was thrown into this well.

He suffered injury in the fall itself. One of his arms was badly injured. One can never say whether it was actually fractured, inasmuch as no medical evidence can be adduced. Then came the unbearable agony of being in close contact with putrid flesh. Wherever he reached in the darkness he came into contact with these rotting bodies. He found that even prayer was very hard under the circumstances. The iron lid of the well was securely locked after he had been thrown in, plunging the whole well into complete darkness. How he survived more than a few hours of this torture is hard to imagine.

Nearly two days elapsed where breathing itself was so difficult and Sundar knew he was nearing the end. As he prayed he heard a grating sound on the iron door of the well. It was the third night and someone was opening the door of the well. Presently there was a rope with a loop at its end, which was lowered into the well, and he was asked to hold it tight. With his one good arm, as well as he could, he clung to the rope, having thrust a leg into the loop. Gently he was raised to the top of the well. His visitors shut the door and locked it and before he could thank them they were gone! Once again, without a doubt, these were angelic visitors. The key to the door itself hung from the girdle around the waist of the chief lama and was not available to any other person. In this marvellous way God released His servant so that he could continue his unrelenting labours.

It took some doing to rid his yellow robe of the stench of putrid flesh. Having washed and dried his clothes clean, Sundar Singh proceeded back to the market square, where, to the astonishment of everybody, he began to preach. One can imagine the consternation and the absolute sensation that his reappearance, after he was taken for dead in the well, should have made upon the onlookers. It was not long before the news reached the head lama and he was once again arraigned before him, in the same hall where he had earlier been condemned to die. It was quite incomprehensible to the lama and all concerned, when there was but one key to the door of the well and it hung on the key ring beneath the lama's robes, how Sundar could have gained his release from the well. The upshot of this inexplicable miracle was that the head lama ordered Sundar Singh to be thrust out of the town with the injunction that he was never to set foot in it again.

The sheer joy evinced by Sundar Singh when under extreme pain and third degree torture, had a tremendous impact upon all his persecutors. To them, his joy and the whole-hearted thanksgiving to Jesus, which he incessantly gave, were solid rebukes and sure darts to their darkened consciences.

16

In the Heavenlies

There have been just a very select few who enjoyed communion with God which literally took them into the heavenlies. There was John, in the Island of Patmos, communing with the Lord Jesus Christ with a closeness of intimacy which few men have ever known. Then there was St. Paul, who, in the twelfth chapter of 2 Corinthians, wrote in the third person about himself, "I knew a man in Christ . . . (whether in the body, I cannot tell; or whether out of the body, I cannot tell: God knoweth;) such an one caught up to the third heaven . . . and heard unspeakable words, which it is not lawful for a man to utter" (vs. 2,4). St. Francis of Assisi was yet another whose communion with God appeared to be quite out of this earth.

While Sundar Singh was chary about revealing these intimate experiences of his communion with God, he somehow managed to

disclose—whether wittingly or unwittingly—
that almost on a regular basis he would get
carried into the very presence of God. His body,
no doubt, would remain still in the attitude of
prayer, but in spirit he would be walking in the
heavenlies and conversing with his Lord and
Master. Some have called this experience 'going
into ecstasy'. Of course, this expression has its
limitations. After a long time he would return to
find that quite a few hours had elapsed. He
began to use great caution and restraint lest
being suddenly taken up in this fashion, he
would return to find that it was too late to keep
his speaking appointments. It is not on record
that he missed any meeting on this account.

It is not to be wondered at, that many who
could not understand some of his experiences
such as going into ecstasy and also his other
mystic experiences, criticized him. As a matter of
fact, Sundar Singh must have expected to be
misunderstood. After all, which true disciple of
Jesus was not criticized and belittled?

We are living in times today when a very
large preponderance of Christians scarcely know
how to pray for five minutes. Many who wanted
to 'investigate' and study this new 'Superstar'

Sundar Singh, were simply not in the same league or 'class' with him and therefore could hardly understand him. Here was simplicity itself—a Christlike simplicity of faith in operation.

God granted Sundar Singh also to see a great personal victory in the conversion of his dear dad who had initially suffered much pain and embarrassment at Sundar's conversion to Christ. His dad approached him saying, "I want to be baptized by you." But Sundar Singh said, "No, you must be ready to be baptized in the Name of Jesus Christ by any true Christian preacher." What a joy it was to Sundar Singh to see the triumph of the Gospel in his own father's life!

On one occasion, while Sundar was a guest in the house of a simple Christian, a money order arrived from his father. It was a large sum of money which his dad had sent him. When the postman came with the money order, Sundar just signed the money order form and handed over the money to his host. Thus to the end of his life, Sundar remained true to his convictions, to possess nothing and carry no currency. His father who had a touching concern and love for him continued sending him some help from time to time, though Sundar's own personal needs were but few.

17

Sundar Singh's Western Tours

Soon after his conversion, Sundar Singh began to develop a deep longing to tread the very paths that the Lord Jesus in His lifetime trod. But his application for passport was turned down to his great disappointment. Thus it was that he turned his feet to the incredibly dangerous regions of Baluchistan and of the North-west Frontier Province. When the British rulers carved Pakistan out of the Indian sub-continent, on the obdurate and intransigent demands of the Moslem leader, Ali Mohammed Jinnah, these almost ungovernable regions, populated by turbulent and trigger-happy tribesmen, fell within the borders of the new country.

Many years passed before God gave Sundar Singh the great desire of his heart. As a man well-known and renowned for his godliness, he travelled to Europe and addressed meetings in several cities of Switzerland, England, and in the United States. Sundar Singh, however, seemed to have suffered much in the materialistic atmosphere of the West where he felt very stifled, almost to the point of suffocation. It is understandable that, to one who had laboured so long under the mistaken notion that the West was largely Christian, the real picture would have come as a dreadful shock. Further, for one who had grown in spirit in the solitude and quietness of the Himalayas, the greed, the avid pursuit of money and things and the resultant neglect of the Lord Jesus must have been very trying, to say the least.

It was in Singapore that he preached in English for the first time, when there was no one to translate for him from Hindustani to English.

In England a very striking incident took place. Sundar Singh called at the home of a vicar. The maid who answered the knock on the vicar's door, stood aghast. She neither welcomed him inside, nor intimated her master about the visitor at the door. Finally the vicar called out, "Mary, who is at the door?" "Sir", she answered, "I cannot say who is at the door if it is not the Lord Jesus!" The vicar came and found that Sundar Singh was at the door. He struck people as a Christlike man, yet he was so unpretentious and sought only to exalt his Lord and Master.

18

The Last Journey

To those of us who daily check the day's temperature and in certain climes listen carefully to the weather forecast so that we know what kind of weather one has to face, what clothes to wear, and what hazards of the road to expect, the exploits of Sundar Singh are hopelessly beyond our mental depths. How did he, this intrepid young man, cross the highest mountain passes in the world and walk barefoot on eternal snows! Sometimes his feet did bleed and he gained the title, "The apostle with the bleeding feet."

As Sundar Singh prepared for the last of his Tibetan journeys, seeing his poor health his friends tried to prevail upon him, to set aside his plans. But Sundar was adamant. He must go. This was the special mission field to which he was called—Tibet. Poor health and the dangers along the way would never deflect him from the path of duty.

Thus he set out never to return. How far he penetrated into Tibet on this last occasion in 1929, one can never say. My dad, however, would say, "Sundar Singh walked so close to heaven that God could have easily caught him up, as He caught up Elijah." It is just as well that there is no gravestone with a high sounding epitaph, where men would repair to pay him respects. If such a location had ever been designated, it would have become a shrine and a place of pilgrimage where men's veneration might have exceeded all legitimate bounds. And in a land so full of idolatry, there would have arisen large sections of men and women who would have brought candles to light or offerings to such a shrine! All this would have been a total negation of all Sundar Singh stood for—for he had taught men to love Jesus with all their hearts and live like Him and never hesitate to be partakers of His sufferings.

19

Some Gripping Insights

In his letters to intimate friends, Sundar gave certain deep insights and penetrating observations from his many journeys. A few of them will help to widen our understanding.

Depth and faith usually come with trials. Some of his Himalayan and Tibetan experiences make us wonder at the power of God that could make Sundar endure, where ordinary mortals weakened by fear, would scarcely have survived.

Of Lao on the bare wind-swept plateau of Tibet he wrote: "At a height of 16,000 feet we slept out in the open . . . The cold was so intense that all feeling went out of the body. We became numb all over. The whole of one night the rain fell in torrents and in the bitter cold we had to sit all night under an umbrella. This place is a very dangerous one, for many people have died in the snow.

"On the 15th of July, we came to Hampu La Pass which is nearly 19,000 feet high, where we saw the corpses of three men who had died from the terrible cold. At this great height we could scarcely draw our breath; our hearts and lungs were filled with pain and the beating of our hearts sounded in our ears. Here is a great glacier in which many people have lost their lives and their bodies have never been recovered till this day. Thanks be to God we passed through this awful place in safety.

"On 16th July we arrived at a Tibetan village, Mutth, where the headman received us kindly and that night he invited an important lama to dine with us. He understood Hindustani and we preached the Word. He listened with great attention and pleasure and did not prevent others from hearing also. The next day we went on and preached in every place we passed through."

In England, although he found himself considerably restricted by his lack of fluency in English, he found many who received his message.

A lady in whose house he had lived, wrote, "It is wonderful having Sundar Singh here; it is unlike anything else that has happened; it is indescribable, but it is like having Christ in the house as near as we could imagine what that could be like."

At Oxford University, although he was subjected to much critical scrutiny, there were many who spoke of having been greatly blessed by his visit. A student said, "As I heard him I thought I was hearing Christ." A member of the faculty said, "He reminds us of the apostolic age." A clergyman, who attended a special meeting for priests and clergy, said that he was so blessed and remarked, "I could have kissed his feet." Rather a strange thing for an Englishman to say!

Even when Sundar Singh was labouring in the cities of China, the call of Tibet seemed to be quite strong upon his heart. In fact, he wanted to enter Tibet directly from China. He, in fact, revealed this desire in a letter to a friend, one Mr. Popley, with whom he had close fellowship. Mr. Popley was a missionary of the London Missionary Society working at Erode in South India. So close were the bonds between them

that he even wrote: "Please don't write 'Sadhuji'*
to me. I am your little brother in Christ. I shall be
glad if you will write 'little brother' instead of
'Sadhuji'."

In yet another letter from China, Sundar said
to Mr. Popley, "I have been in Shanghai and
Nanking, and from here I am going to . . .
Peking. I wanted to go to Tibet from China but
now it is quite impossible because the Chinese
are fighting with the Tibetans. So now I have to
come back to India and then go back to
Tibet . . ."

After preaching in Japan in 1919 he had this
observation to make, which in a much greater
measure, applies to the Japan of today. Sundar
seemed to think that Japanese victories in the
battlefield and in the other fronts had shattered
the foundations of their spiritual life. He said,
"Japan has plunged herself in the soul-killing
floods of Western materialism. Her eyes are
filled with visions of worldly greatness. She is in
the fury of making money and has no ear for the
Word of God . . . In my conversation with her
leaders, I drew attention to the growing
immorality in the country." He felt sad that

*'ji' is a suffix which denotes profound respect.

moral awareness and repugnance of evil was badly dented by the strong push for material advancement.

Sundar saw a contrast in the prevailing scene in the China of that day. He found certain leaders and even army generals to be professing Christians. He therefore thought that it was a great deal more socially acceptable, for one to follow the Lord Jesus in China, than in Japan. He wrote, "With regard to students, there is a danger of testing Christianity among them by the number of pledge cards (decision cards) they sign. I don't much believe in it. When I addressed a meeting in China, nearly all the students present signed cards promising to study the claims of Christ. I know enough of human nature to believe that not more than one hundredth of them will be able to keep the promise . . . All things considered, the Chinese are more open . . . than the Japanese." The validity of some of these observations is true to a great measure even to this day.

But the following incident shows that the Japanese were not totally insensitive to the Saviour. Sundar Singh happened to be visiting a girls' high school in Osaka. A girl who beheld him pass, ran into the Principal's office and shouted, "Teacher, teacher, here comes Jesus. His Christlike demeanour was not lost upon the people of this country.

Thus it is hard to say how many lives Sundar Singh influenced just by the briefest interaction with them. Wherever he went impulses of a life-changing nature proceeded from him. That indeed is an abiding quality of those who walk humbly with the Lord.

Plotting Sundar's Place in History

At the turn of the twentieth century, Europe and England were getting flooded with modernistic teaching which debunked the authority of the Bible and referred to most of the books of the Bible as comprising merely of myths and fables. There were strident voices across the globe which spoke of wanting to demythologize the Bible. These men, in fact, were plunging seminaries and churches into complete darkness. At such a time when faith was at a low ebb and people felt lost as to what to believe, God chose to raise a simple Indian boy—and a most unlikely person at that—to bring to bear on sane people's consciousness that Jesus who rose again from the dead, is still ALIVE today and that He is "the Saviour of the world".

Standing before an august company of

erudite professors and students at Oxford, Sundar Singh declared with unbounded assurance and certainty, "I know whom I have believed, and am persuaded that he is able to keep that which I have committed unto him against that day" (2 Timothy 1:12). Wherever he went, men returned to faith in the Lord Jesus. If Christianity had appeared rather impractical and abstract, it was no longer so, after Sundar Singh burst on the scene.

Sundar Singh was not just a star but a constellation. With his simplicity and his face aglow with love, he seemed to reflect the beauty of the Risen Christ to the extent to which earthly vessels can contain and reflect Him.

To those who, like the present writer's late father, were earnestly seeking to glorify Jesus and longing to see first century Christianity, Sundar Singh brought an immense fillip to their faith and strength to their aspirations. The tremendous encouragement Sundar Singh was to the writer's late dad,* when the latter was still in his teens, was borne out through a half a century of soul-winning and demonstrating the

*You can read that inspiring account in the book, "Another Daniel" by the same author.

Risen Christ.

While most men of our modern day major more in activity somehow-or-other related in some remote way to Christianity, rather than any actual pursuit of Christ Himself, you, dear reader, had better set your heart to seek, find, and follow the Lord Jesus Christ who alone brings meaning, purpose, and hope into otherwise drab and boring lives.

By the same author:

Another Daniel

Get Set . . . Go

Pressing Forward

Revival Secrets

Run to Win

Climbing Higher

Breaking through to Victory

Victory over Demons and Fear

John Wesley—Apostle of England

Enslaved Yet Made Free

Mao and Marx Bound Us . . .

"Another Daniel"

by Joshua Daniel

An exciting biography of Mr. N. Daniel, a man who walked with God.

This book is a classic on revival giving a graphic account of the great revival that swept over the Indian Christian scene in the forties, fifties and sixties, in fulfilment of Sundar Singh's prophecy concerning the ministry of Mr. N. Daniel, the present writer's father.

This book presents marvellous vistas of the outpouring of God's Spirit in revival.

Rarely has a reader missed in its pages the quickening, the reviving and the sanctifying voice of the Holy Spirit.

Our Monthly Magazine

CHRIST IS VICTOR

One reader from U.K. writes:

"CHRIST IS VICTOR"

has been my consistent guide to my
Christian life and continually brought me back to
the roots of the Word of God and prayer.

You can keep in touch with the fast-moving
developments as they occur and also
receive a stimulating and enriching
message given by the author.

For further help and blessing
Go to our worldwide web:

www.lefi.org